THE SEAS ARE
DOLPHINS' TEARS

Critical praise for
Djelloul Marbrook's poetry

The Seas Are Dolphins Tears (2018, Leaky Boot Press)

A 21st-century Blake—reconciling innocence and experience—Marbrook urges the contemporary reader to retreat to the quiet of unknowing, to live "in dusks of mirrors," where our truest selves can find their reflections.

—Dean Kostos, Benjamin Saltman Award for *This Is Not a Skyscraper*

Far from Algiers (2008, Kent State University Press)

... as succinct as most stanzas by Dickinson... an unusually mature, confidently composed first poetry collection.

—Susanna Roxman, *Prairie Schooner* (author of *Crossing the North Sea*)

... brings together the energy of a young poet with the wisdom of long experience.

—Edward Hirsch, Guggenheim Foundation

... honors a lifetime of hidden achievement.

—Toi Derricotte, Stan and Tom Wick Poetry Prize judge, author of *Tender* and *The Undertaker's Daughter*

... wise and flinty poems outfox the Furies of exile, prejudice, and longing... a remarkable and distinctive debut.

—Cyrus Cassells, National Poetry Series winner

Brash Ice (2014, Leaky Boot Press, UK)

... a precision that occasionally recalls Yeats ...

—James Polk, *The Country and Abroad*

... aesthetically pleasing, thematically intriguing ...

—Michael Young, *The Poetry*

Brushstrokes and Glances (2010, Deerbrook Editions)

Whether it is commentary on state power, corporate greed, or the intensely personal death of a loved one, Djelloul Marbrook is clear-sighted, eloquent, and precise. As the title of the collection suggests, he uses the lightest touch, a collection of fragments, brushstrokes and glances, to fashion poems that resonate with truth and honesty.

—Phil Constable, *New York Journal of Books*

... looks at art the way a drinker drinks—deeply, passionately, and desperately, as if his life depended on it ... makes you want to run out to your favorite museum and look again, as you have never looked before, until the lights go out.

—Barbara Louise Ungar, author of
Thrift; *Charlotte Bronte, You Ruined My Life*; *The Origin of the Milky Way*

... one of those colossal poets able to bridge worlds—poetry and art, heart and mind—with rare wit, grace, and sincerity; a soft-spoken artist with the courage to face the "fatal beckoning" of his muse ... crisp intellect, seamlessly interwoven with loss and longing.... poetry at its best: at once both gritty and refined, private and political, tender and tough as iron ... well worth reading.

—Michael Meyerhofer, author of
What to do if you're buried alive, Damnatio Memoriae, Blue Collar Eulogies

...delicately wrought... highly recommended reading...because, ultimately, this witness so clearly loves his subject.

—Eileen Tabios, Editor, *Galatea Resurrects*

Riding Thermals to Winter Grounds (2017, Leaky Boot)

... some very powerful lines, such as: "And then, near the end of my life, I become the man I wanted to be without the fuss and bother of giving a damn."

—Sidney Grayling, Editor, Onager Editions

ᕉᕉ

Critical praise for
Djelloul Marbrook's fiction

Artemisia's Wolf (title story, *A Warding Circle*, 2017, Leaky Boot)

... Djelloul Marbrook's impressive novella ... successfully blends humor and satire (and perhaps even a touch of magic realism) into its short length ... an engrossing story, but what might strike the reader most throughout the book is its infusion of breathtaking poetry ... a stunning rebuke to notoriously misogynist subcultures like the New York art scene, showing us just how hard it is for a young woman to be judged on her creative talent alone.

—Tommy Zurhellen, *Hudson River Valley Review*

Saraceno

Djelloul Marbrook writes dialogue that not only entertains with an intoxicating clickety-clack, but also packs a truth about low-life mob culture "The Sopranos" only hints at. You can practically smell the anisette and filling-station coffee.

—Dan Baum, author of *Gun Guys* (2013), *Nine Lives: Mystery, Magic, Death and Life in New Orleans* (2009), and others

...a good ear for crackling dialogue ... I love Marbrook's crude, raw music of the streets. The notes are authentic and on target ...

—Sam Coale, *The Providence* (RI) *Journal*

... an entirely new variety of gangster tale ... a Mafia story sculpted with the most refined of sensibilities from the clay of high art and philosophy ... the kind of writer I take real pleasure in discovering ... a mature artist whose rich body of work is finally coming to light.

—Brent Robison, editor, *Prima Materia*

Alice Miller's Room (title story, *Making Room,* 2017, Leaky Boot)

Marbrook lets his powerful imagination run wild, leading the fiction into unexpected corners where weird performers hold court and produce endings that both astonish and are frequently magical.

—James Polk, contributing editor, *Art/World*

This enchanting novella is a delicately wrought homage to Jung's famous principle of meaningful coincidence...

—*Breakfast All Day,* UK

... the story draws us into that mysterious and terrifying realm where the heart will have its say and all who enter leave transformed...

—Dr. Patricia L. Divine, Head Start program national award winner

Mean Bastards Making Nice (2014, Leaky Boot)

I love it. I admire it. It is you at your best.

—Novelist Gail Godwin on "The Pain of Wearing Our Faces"

Guest Boy (2018, Leaky Boot)

... it is in books like this that I seek answers and guidance as I travel my own path to enlightenment and contentment. This book opened a struggle in me...

—Isla McKetta, editor, *A Geography of Reading*

THE SEAS ARE DOLPHINS' TEARS

poems by

Djelloul Marbrook

LEAKY BOOT PRESS

THE SEAS ARE DOLPHINS' TEARS
by Djelloul Marbrook

First published in 2018 by
Leaky Boot Press
http://www.leakyboot.com

Acknowledgments

This book was first published in slightly different form in 2016
as *Shadow of the Heron* (now out of print) from
Coda Crab Books, Seattle, WA.

"Woodstock" first appeared in *Fledgling Rag* No. 10, April 2011.

"After image" first appeared in *Pirene's Fountain*, April 2013.

"The creatures zanies see in him" (then titled "Shape memory") and
"That first kiss" first appeared in *Le Zaparogue* No. 9 (France),
December 2010.

ISBN: 978-1-909849-60-0

Author's Acknowledgments

Endless thanks are owed to my wife, Marilyn, who has in so many ways made all my work possible, to James Goddard, my publisher, whose steadfast faith in my work brought it to light and buoyed me in rough waters, to Sebastien Doubinsky who published my work and introduced me to James Goddard, to Brent Robison, whose wizardly videos and deft hand with e-books still astonish us; to Kevin Swanwick, whose radiance as a reader and advisor unfailingly enlightens me, and to Emily Brooks, whose artistic taste, good cheer and resourcefulness seem fathomless.

For Raymond N. Nelson
and Miles Cunningham

The Sigh of Compassion flows through the things of the world like the waters of a river and is unceasingly renewed.

The world is God's shadow.

—*Ibn al 'Arabi*

Contents

proem

detained by naked angels

he goes a-viking

leviathan sobs

his lenses are children's tears

he sails away on a slice of apple

evensong

coda

proem

something superior to breath

I

hope runs in running water
to where it doesn't matter
a court of dolphins waits
to humor us to order
this atlantis of remembrance

I run in silvery threads
unraveling memories
& threading them
impulse to element
superior to breath

II

Why do dolphins make us smile?
What do they weave in water
but the fabric of mirth? We imagine
riding them and like to think
they might be smarter than we are,
a concession we grant very few.

What about them makes our day,
jollies us, encourages us to go on
to ends we can't prescribe? We might
even acquiesce to their rule, except
they might find it a primitive idea.
Do we smile because they like us?

III

What sort of family would you have preferred?
Dolphins reassuring ferries of the dead
there are no final crossings, but not this
orphanage that makes so many sacrifices
out of love—dolphins understand
hypocrisy better than a child,
and if they look as if they're laughing
it's only not to panic fools.
You were not so foolish as to prefer simple honesty then?
No, I should have been waterborne.
I never trusted surfaces not to tilt
or a question to harbor decent intent.

IV

Sailors have premonitions
about icebergs, whales and squalls
and so do I upon the seas
of my routine madnesses.

If I navigate around them
it's only to encounter spouts
or dragons rearing
from suckholes' panic.

I know about torn sails,
cracked tangs and bad luck
and the homeport on my transom
is a figment and illusion.

There is no setting out,
no homecoming—boats
do not belong upon the sea
as much as dangers do.

The sea is the dolphins' tears:
how dare we be angry
racing our conceits
for a dollar's worth of grief?

detained by naked angels

detained by naked angels

and then you will be taken to naples
           where you will be photographed
           in all the usual impositions
after which you will be interrogated
           by two naked florentine angels
           who will interpret your silences
to signify the outcome of your mission
           and the degree to which you remember
           why you consented to be captured
and then you will begin your ascent
           stripped of your pretensions
           allotted one memory of our tumult here

he exiles his shadow

what sort of creatures have friends?
none who wear this kind of face

the missus is not stuck on the cardinal
but she is stuck with him, and i,
trying to cast no shadow, obsess
like a heron about the position of the sun,
fishing for someone else's friends

i'm full of crop circles and nazca lines,
mazes of nothing exactly where it was—
where in such a world would friends
fit in exactly, where would I stow them
among such enigmas, where when *there*
is the most elusive word I know?
answers are bound to rid us of friends

i have no faith anything will be
where i left it, no faith in promises
of shape, size, scent and other marks
of recognition   only this record-keeping,
these equations erased at night,
assure me that when i look down
to crack an oyster these lines will make sense

for now i know if the sun warms a heron's back
the fish will see his shadow   my strategy
is different   i look behind you for your shadow
not because you have long teeth,

such people being common,
but because angels have no shadow,
although we're more attracted to vampires

i used to avoid men who looked like me,
i didn't think i could bring them around
to talk of inconsequential things

here's what i made of their hawkish looks,
that they would sit all night on pilings listening
to the exhalation of deceits

no one panders to such intent
or breaks the concentration
of one who has no doubts

such men cast no shadow
even if the sun insists they do—
they will know when to roll up my own

he awakes

the city came unglued from the globe
when the lineman made love to the waitress
and the boy pretended to watch bluegills
having seen the apocalypse and knowing
books cannot ballast the dizzying world

his plea

do not harm me
such a simple request
and yet caged in a parenthesis
i rattle its impossibility

do not harm me
as if i had the right
to such audacity as if
the words do not erase themselves

do not as if
i could enter a parenthesis
and survive the cyclotron
of expectations

survive meteor rains
world-making tampering
with each other
that is our harm and wish for pain

do not wish me
here there or anything
lest you cut your fingers
on the mystery

premonition

i fly out from cactus
to prowl old thought's belly
and come upon the bones
of hopes picked clean
by carrion eaters whom
i loved and now i liquor up
on alien milk and dread
of finding forensic evidence
of my connivance here
evidence i sailed this sea
of tears before it parched
and came to owlish grief
because i could not read
my sealed orders' gibberish

qualm

what's life but datum
and buoy waiting for us
chiming on the far side of storm?

nothing is left behind
the days are hurtling overhead
to await us in disguise

i know a little more than this
but may need it to perfume
this or that available body

writing names

for each of us a pantheon
of gods who betrayed us

write their names on river stones
cross them out with water

smooth when they troubled us
smoother now they don't

think of them as loot
to buy a well-forged visa

he sets out

i'm turning out not to be him
the body that got me here
such wrath splattered on it
he should hang in a glass case
in a darkened armory
with moose elk and artifacts
of the rich and brightly pained
i have stepped out on him
and taken a bus to this somewhere
memories do not smell of naptha

departing prayer

i would like to go up in a balloon
up to the balloonable reaches of up
to parachute my fancies down
on billowy hills of décolletage
like to reach up to reach down
basketing me risibly riding word balloons
in the comic air and seeding
ebbing days with recognitions
eating up my clothes
like this like that likely to disappear
before i have time to take me seriously

he glances back

there he is his topiary head
jollying doorways and doubters
in sepia brooklyn running boards
coney island and whooping cough

a pudgy little guy who never would
play his cards well or suit
anyone's idea of belonging
sorry in his wicker stroller

for being there or anywhere
apologetic for what he wouldn't
ever be able to figure out
but would die many times trying

breyer's wagons butterflies
evening flowers delight him
but what to do about him
no woolen leggings warm

too solemn him for them
gaze too wide and sticky
too altogether too that
they are prepared to fear

then he follows the sun

heliotrope born in the shade
not much i hold out for you
but hallelujahs of fingertips
touching finials in the dark
not much but oily daisies
and blasts of farting trucks
piss of roaming creatures
dry wells and power outs
for heliotropes born in shade
blood draws and prognosis
failure of solar systems
and a thousand eyes staring
at a blue optometrist's ear

he goes a-viking

he goes a-viking

sea foam of vowels
consonants glistening
oar words to illogic
dragons and dread
to go a-viking
with shield maidens
on saracen isles
to kill rape sack
grow tea roses
lay loot aboard
blazing verbs again
to scandinavias
of grindels and sumbels

from the fury of words
good lord deliver us
from their honings
bludgeonings and loss
how can we strip them
straighten their gaze
not to humiliate
but to exhort them
to lead the child out
from torches and clangor
down to the sea
where the longships wait
for a tortuous rowing
to an honorable place

for a crack at the sublime

cartwheel compasses and faces
lose your polarity and swing
overture to opera unseeing
across the empty quarter
projections haunt

i have come here grieving
none could assuage
but faces in passing trains
and snapshots of the dead

grieving
       come here
            you

swing to true north on my forehead
to know you are where
oh yes let there be where
somewhere yet to go
and not these faces
in arctic snow

let there be a there and it
or at least a buoy gong
and fog not garroting it
at least a familiar sound
in this chill whatness

what

what's not dangerous to take
including this or that meaning
what's good for us is not
for whom we sniff around
and who is scouting us
for a crack at the sublime

particle me your saturn
tide me over your moon
i will steady your axis
eclipse your astonishment
be wholly bad for you
just to take my medicine

the moon is walking backwards
a full moon is bad mojo
like us shining on each other
from our secret gardens

shining
      pulling
            letting go

despising candor to distill
the odors ardors of the mind
so not to die of our deceits
too musky thick and slow
we should change our clothes
after snitching hellebore
and other dangers
from each other's gardens
should sober up and speak
of our misadventures
in the calyxes and pistils
and stamens of the night

secret no not as much
as our compassed faces
what do they say gravityless
for all the shirking
and pussyfooting around
say we've had too much to say
in the wolfy teeth of evidence
we're high as kites
on our misdeeds

panic

metabolically speaking
dying since day one
makes a laundry list
a deathbed confession
and i think licenses us
to party on illegal truths
disrupt traffic lights
and fix each other's gaze

is this too much to ask
metabolically speaking
since all we have to lose
is the life we're losing
and can we really trust
such a forlorn question

as for us spinning tops
i notice that the best of us
counterclockwise bear
sea rains to refresh
the brittleness of drought
that ravages our innards

metabolically i'm bound
to starry matters and ignition
of light and projects of the mind
to which i belong in spite
of the occasional delusion and fear
doctor mengele will pick me out
for kindly horrors in the night

metabolically speaking
my polar head is drowning cities
with its b-movie crying jags
and i'm plucking survivors
with my forefinger and thumb
and seating them in business class
to dream of purposes
until their papers come

dank passageways

my mind encrypts my eyes' dispatch
and in this bletchley park i rant
against vainglorious generals
who deny the mind is boobied
to blast important men away

my mind encrypts raw sensations
to cache them behind bricks
in dank trickling passageways
because ponce de leons become
uncontainable and savage

night vision

my mirror neurons note
your navel's looking away
but somehow your crotch
is making eye contact
with the molested girl
who haunts the corridors
of this foreboding place

i can't make this right
but you may scribble
cryptograms in the fog
on my medicine chest
telling me you've decided
to return to your home
in the emerald woods

my night vision goggles
will not find you there
and all that's left of you
will be an entry in a log
that i found fair weather
when i plied the briny sea
of your heaving navel

lost parts

if you never call again
who'll be rid of whom
and where do we bury
the lost parts of us

which manner of speaking
glance or gesture
shall we remember
and yet not die of them

if i cede you this street
that town or room
will you be satisfied
or will you metastasize

falling out

with whom haven't i fallen out
and tumbled down a den
of rattlesnakes

what is left of me
to keep me company
the rest of the way

who will be left to abandon me
or for me to abandon
in such deliberate dark

if you have the answers
there is time to orchestrate
another falling out

eternal bridge repair

county route 6
      the forever road
forgetting there or not
for getting there or not
road of eternal bridge repair
come-to-jesus curves   coydogs
stalking ghosts bounding deer
that look like shoeless lovers
getting where somewhere's not
forever washouts and detours
oily icy county route 6
frequented by vultures black
as the fear there is and is not
on county route 6 angels whisk
us hardly living to slab ends
and quell their desires in the snow

obscene precautions

not the untoward things
according to state law
abide more
than children should have to bear
and under any circumstances
especially these about which
i may or may not speak later
wash their hands
and be especially careful
to treat patrons as if
to supply the proper words
they were microbes
so voracious that precautions
delay the last train
to where we have always feared
while at dangerous crossings
we beguiled
make out in back seats
wait for something to happen
which in every instance just did
while we were looking
in store windows and at fastballs
yes momma was a fastball
dad a cutter and i
believe instructions
should be posted on those behinds
i have been glad to see walk away

must
take obscene precautions
to forget where any home is
because should be is always
an illusion on the grand isle
in someone's navel

lost in the midst of finding

what did you think would happen
if you missed this appointment
some nameless catastrophe
which is of course my name
without the middle initial
which if i had one would be
a clue to what might happen
if i followed my natural wont
to get lost in the midst of finding
goodbye hello neighborhoods
i know not more than once a day
in the heart of such familiarity
i cannot find my way
one must be one's own light
in cracks between ordinariness
and exquisite punishments
waiting to be meted out
to those who arrive too late
having become lost en route
to where one supposes one has been

his shadow deserts

and they never came back
because they had never been there
who encouraged me to call there here

and if they had come back
would the mirrors have affirmed it
would the ground beneath my feet hold firm

or would i topple over
not in love but to hold them
as if it were up to me to give them substance

and who would this me be
taking responsibility for ditchers
waiting for them to come back to somewhere

words flee

so much loveliness after me
i don't care about them anymore
words like painted buntings flee
to warmer sentences
no one fills the room
the way those narcissists do
no one papers me to walls
because now my grievances
quit their consonants
and ride fiery vowels to sea

does this happen in afghanistan
loveliness after reptilian minds
come and go in private jets
blowing smoke in our eyes
happen to remember warblers
after so many words
dollars rubles spent
may paper cuts on private parts
shingles and cocktails
of contaminants await them

on their arrival in washington
and all the porticos of sepsis
could leave a better world
if words did not run red
on contact with the air

if methane did not leak
from political endeavor
if we could die assured
of so much loveliness after us
i could simply shut my mouth

to be a smoldering window

i am the hole in the air
through which my country 'tis of thee
sends smoke signals
to the stupefied of jupiter
on nightclub roofs
& i none too siriusly
butterfly valve fluttering
rid myself of knowledge
in my shell-shocked sleep
while the night train rattles
carrying me to all those dachaus
otherwise known as backroom memories
the kind employees swill
as antidotes to patrons

i am myself an antidote
to what was promised me
beliefs or cures or conventions
that could not prevent me
from becoming this
through which you rise
flag-drenched and drunk
to become bugsquash   on the windshield
of that 13th world   our heartbeats herald

i am ready for it   wind shapes me
to accommodate you   your dread hospitals
and political shapes   i am ready
and if not me   another hole in the air

i am the hoop of fire
through which the vaudeville dog
declines to jump
& you & your constitutional rights
clamor like glitter   in the summer air

i am the smoldering window
through which your furniture
and your parents hurtle   i am the vagina
in which the cosmos   thinking no more of you
than a ruby in a meteorite   i am all that i became
considering what you thought
                                            becoming

leviathan sobs

he forgets

how to die enough for them
or imagine for them being dead
or be dead enough for them

their breath is foul wind
their dreams ill-makers
i haven't swamp to strain

moraine and seep
push me up to bob
in gray morose beds

leviathan

these sobs rise from leviathan
tortured beast
    and i in every one of them
tortured beast
    breach the moonstruck surface
celebrating
    the crime from which i come

leviathan sobs
    at the bottom of the sea
        & sends up his little children
            who look like me
            & once inhabited
                chapters of my book
wearing all the faces
    i have worn
        to greet this star and that
encased
    in glassy antisepsis
        of grief
navigating
    petri dishes
        in which climates
            & cultures storm

        these sobs punctuate
    galaxies of sentences
with periods
    potential
        as novas

leviathan at the bottom of the sea
when you sob
  remember me
    remember that
tortured beasts
  thrash beneath
    every sorrow
      & imprisoned thing
tortured beasts
  beyond the reach
    of penance poking
messages
  from this muck
    in the countless eyes
      of god
heretical
  innocent
    undismayed

he would just like to say

i would just like to say
i'm sure you would
we've heard enough
of what you would
and we are gathered here
to keep there there   to keep
outside out   inside in
& pay tribute to
life-threatening conditions
germs & nanobots
partying in our nooks
cruising in our crannies
waiting for us outside
where we think we live
in our confusion
tripping over trinkets
triumphs & nonesuch
is our loony lot
lightning-lit and struck
with inscrutable directions
hoorahs & harrumphs
boogaloos bugaboos & bumps

his apartment

apartment for rent
to keep us apart
as if we're not apart
too much apartment
to let as if we let
anything get in the way
of our apartment

nor will flowery hats
and crumby beards
rescue us from what
if we truly were
different from
the ones we wish
to differ from

what others default
how can we occupy
laugh and fuck
& generally pretend
our parents suck
more than we do
or rent that's due

e-mail invitation

hi can we meet
and the evils thereof
in a heavenly video
and fondle the possibilities
of a strained relationship
between alien beasts

can we cavort in the aviaries
of the spluttering stars
and sting each other
in the vaulted apiaries
of our pretensions
and will you buy a vial

of a mere excretion
of so heavenly a body
the moon would rather wane
than gaze upon it
by which i mean
an ordinary decency

evil nurse

sun is an evil nurse
(look at her fingers)
and when i am gone
i will have sought asylum
among beasts
sketched by stars

thermals of her quim
will lift me up to sirius
and i will swear
i would be tortured
if i fell down
to the sweaty briar
of her designs on me

i will tell angels
wearing remembered faces
of darting room to room
to escape orderlies
who held me down for her
& i will forget to sob

he is a woman

in this game of hurdles
set down in briar the wicked run
but i have lost my shoes
and bleed among diamonds

my clit is in my throat
sputtering with glee
i am burning up the air
they need to finish

who hip-bumped me
and sent me end over end
into the beery crowd
a defusable IED

see how i must be capitalized
or you wouldn't know
the finishing line isn't always
where you think it is

he eludes the booleans

google aka god sent an algorithm
to collect me for the specimen case
on planet x where they're studying
ideology's effects on the human brain

none of the engines coughed me up
even the booleans could not find me
there was not even a soiled sheet
no body no crime just this golem

searching forlornly for its double
boozy with the emissions
of the heron-flapping equation
carrying off its name and reason

and tries to sing

this one his pettiness
that one his nobility
the burdens onerous
no song without silence

he placates jupiter

i am crossing out jalool
leaving his facsimile
to fool his relativities
and stretch the night
that truth be glimpsed
through the moth holes
imagining that it is
something like a home
where you close your eyes

something crawls beneath
and scurries overhead
but in the next room
parents sleep and outside
trees count their leaves
i rock the selves i put to sleep
prop a chair against the door
not sure they will awake
                              or should

and pours a poem

bloody silence comes to boil
the pot is lifted by its ears
to pour a poem upon the page

i thought silence is the page
on which the word is written,
but this is mad and riotous

he asks words to step aside

(for max picard, 1888-1965)

i don't know enough to say anything
the silence this induces
is what i know of art

i must ask words to step aside
so that i may measure all
i don't have to say

noise is cozening rape
thuggee of the state
tattooed with lies

they get over themselves

there wasn't much to say after that
and i've forgotten what that was
for all the pretending it never was
and this is how words get over themselves
by wiping their little mouths on their ties
and stomping past the other drunken lords

my look is made of visitors' smiles
that suck the this from that and spin
young boys off the edge of cliffs
dizzy with the hallowedeness of a glance
and after that all there is to say
will be mumbled to the wrong person

his lenses are children's tears

salt

the horse ate the steering wheel
   for the salt of the driver's hand
      i wish my sins were as funny

the horse and i had our reasons
   two big heads barging in a window
      turning a wheel to a boning knife

why his memories glisten

when i don't let a body rest
but stage it in my mind
i know blindness at midday
follows such a matinée

let all my memories glisten
in children's tears
nannies and terrorists
cannot wipe away

we are not the age we think
ancient medieval modern
no we are most of all
what we think we've lost

and all this is the glare
that blinds us to each other
out from under the marquee
of our fey nickelodeons

thrall of glass

whose mind does not distort the spectrum
 of light played upon it   i am low-iron glass
  and yet i amber what comes at me too vividly

glass does not fortress us as mortar does,
 it portends our invisibility   but it suggests
  we are not ready for each other's minds

glass is the most sinister of our inventions
 referring to the left-handedness of things
  the glories of contrariness and bastardy

glass is the thrall of something contained
 the illusion of seeing through anything
  a melancholy and lovely testament

that we transmute what we observe
 to wraiths whose love frightens us
  and madnesses too elegant to bear

he rides a paper dish

tar balls and medical debris
slop under the door
down will come baby
cradle and all
ebb beyond reach
of mcmansions galore

ride a paper dish
down the maw of a shark
ride your bed as raft
out to the bloody moon
three sheets to the blast
of monumental apathy

i like the corridors very much
in ms. titan's veins
and am looking forward
to being her exudences
and if that is not the right word
such is the politics of it

the politics of all of it
in this family of disjunctives
throwing tar balls at each other
and calling them snowballs
in the name of trickledown bejesus
and the sweeties he didn't call

on a sea of prejudices

hurtling in their pickup trucks
to keep their appointed prejudices
they anoint with styrofoam and plastic
the invasive green opposing them

at night they bolt the gates
against our heresies and them
oh yes there's always them
to rust the chainsaws

and make the acned daughters
of drunken fathers big
with immigrant leers
and awful possibilities

too populous to think

us madding lumberers
acrawl with creatures yammering
how dare we touch each other
infested as we are
with livelies clamoring

us madding lumberers
whose teeming beasties riot
even in the pores of gods
whose fiery rimworlds streak
wetwoods of dreams

we are too populous to think
too fragrant slumbering
through microbial encounters
to put our wits together
& make anything but scent

he haunts museums

here at this deer crossing
    rednecks chuck beer cans
        and a drunken boy drowned in his own blood

this is the latest nadir
    he haunts museums and reads books
        in a panic to transcend

to escape the amenities

bears and all the other amenities
for the ghoul who has everything
but a country and a life
that's what i call living

in the year of the great oil spill
when even a british accent
has americans worrying
about their spouses' eyeteeth

conundrum

if everything distracts us from something else
does everyone distract us from someone else
and if that something and someone coalesce
the moment may be so exquisite we'll look away

he waits elven tables

if i had a robin's ear and a peregrine's eye
i'd see the rats in the crypts and hear
worms feeding on the received idea

but i think that i would prey on moguls
behind their gates and deposit snakes
on satin spreads and crow about it

jays don't know why redtails screech
but they imitate them   why can't I
wait elven tables under corkscrew willows

attends faerie parties

red sky in the morning
got to get comfortable again
on yet another planet
shed the must of darkened travel
disguise the perfume of my breath
as if my life depended on it
observe with casual lust
pass it off as bonhomie

got to get comfortable again
to sirens and another palette
eerie weather   the usual follies
red sky in the morning
and getting old in time
to cop out on wisdom's perils
and hobble off bum-knee'd
and blind for steel focusing

red sky in the morning
and one too many moons
where i was the night before
the owls were getting used to me
and i could grope through brush
to break onto faerie parties
an endangered guest
                    now i am truly lonely

sees the glory

let me not be born again with such a face
that pages cannot turn without it
that families orbit backwards around it

a face with too much there in it
a destiny a bit too large
for the shoulders and too full
for the the antique and the fey

i don't have the right typeface to write
don't have the right don't know the rite
and am as elegant as a bedouin in his saddle
—my eyes have seen the glory that harms
and may yet incinerate us

questions the parts

what parts of me no longer touchable
are already gone to make another me
for whom the effort to remember you
instead of burning up the years is turning
shit to emeralds and diddling strangers
in their beds to cajole their dreams
from fragrant lairs into the sun's
unforgiving glare—
parts no one has touched
since i was an astonished boy
parts god and women for all their wiles
have not found   they having gone ahead of me
to find you whom i was forced to leave behind

before he got the roses in

this is the world they never got done

it's hard to breathe their remorse

attics remain cluttered   gardens just begun

their whispers deafen me   their loss
beyond religions to console

how smooth the coverlet of the interrupted
how well phragmites hide distress
loosestrife   shattered glass

i pass through dappled cold spots
patted   cajoled to carry messages
and delete the ellipses of the dead
to provide the words that eluded them

the man for whom the algorithm is named
the man who died before he got the roses in
they tried to explain why i should not be sad
but as many prefer their prejudices
i found sorrow comfortable

i found what would grow in it

he sails away on a slice of apple

at a party for his shadow

i'm going to throw a birthday party
for my shadow's efforts to be rid of me
when i can figure out how long it's been
since our collaboration had a purpose

all of you who have enjoyed my shade
put on your sunscreen and come undressed
unblessed and eager to toss around
solar flares and random consequences

i know shadows have solemn missions
they are under no obligation to tell
and i want to give mine a grand send-off
maybe even get a little drunk

because next time i stand before the light
i'm going to be more alone than i've ever been
and without my phony optimism to wear
i'll have to set records between wintry smiles

his face rubs off

summer on earth
as a drunken honey bee
was offered me
i turned it down
to study glaciers
now they're melting

i dock this paper boat
to stone dolphins
of drowned cities
and share my lunch
with peregrines

my face has rubbed off
the pocket change
of illusory friends

i am lost paint
fallen to the floor
from the canvases
of closed museums

i have run out of whim
but recall its bitter taste
and nothing forbidden
tugs or dizzies me
which shaves the serifs
from the alphabet of the end

when i am gone
imagine me
sailing a slice of apple
through an open window
to another possibility

the creatures zanies see in him

my shape-memory runs to filament
and bog light in ruined gardens
so i'm always not quite myself

bacchanalia are stepping stones
over gemmy brooks of dreams
to the creatures zanies see in me

i always look as if i won't
won't this or that or anything
and when i look as if i will

that look of the stooping hawk
makes of zanies snakes and rodents
and humanoids who run away

you can't rivet this contraption
with your electric eyes or strap
it to a table for experiment

because its incarnations
are nothing but your conceits—
it knows itself to be a filament

he aspires to be a needle hole

i am gigantic for this world
putting stars in my hair
dousing comets in my navel
but i don't have to stay here
i have somewhere else to go
don't i look it shilly-shallying
in the corner of your eye
don't worry   i get smaller
as you walk away from me
till i become a needle hole
in your little black dress

rent a villa in tuscany

when i died i rented a villa in tuscany
to spiff up my invented selves
who were oozing from porno shops
and ducking around paragraphs
of recognitions

                         i binged
until it was time to live again and go
to another horror whose embrace
would encourage me to hope

people die slower than things fall apart
but the appearance of slow motion suits us
because we need time to compose our stories
which have a way of composing us

                              but not
letting the child bearing our names recognize us

things fall apart while we pretend they're beginning
and while we orchestrate the artifacts
and string a grid on the ocean's floor
before sending our secrets up in baskets
to die of oxygen and light

                i died of the bends
and needed the order of vineyards
and all that merciless pruning to focus
on a vintage i will never enjoy

see every fancy checked

hieronymus bosch didn't know
we'd be perfect when we're dead
and i don't know it either
but i can see every fancy checked
by forethought and understanding
making heaven a synonym for hell
& so *enjoyment for dummies*
would have to be remaindered

find a grand surprise

who and what to do
anticipating i find
i am myself the grand surprise
waiting in the anticlimax room

a mathematical bum blinded
by an alien scalpel of a poem
i hit the note that cracks
crystal and makes right angles

from which centipedes crawl
and a deadly eccentricity
escapes and leaps hair to hair
across our noble fields

in artemis's underthings

dreaming in artemis's underthings
a coral snake will not pardon my acquisitive hand
the party will grow louder
downstairs beneath the clouds
i will hear the redtail
and one last time
think of bolted rooms
stairs rotting
my intent to whirl dust in light
until i am drafted to sequin angels' gowns

learn what dread is all about

so i'm human after all
disappointment and relief
or half a starry thing
i would settle for
the wonderful trouble
it would bring

false starts vague outs
tasteless as quinoa
wear me down as slowly
as waiting in a room
to be born again
reading grubby magazines

faceless in a room
waiting for a face
wondering whether
to argue about it
or be heroic and learn
what dread is all about

so i'm human after all
the inferences
you're not one of us
you being me us being
anyone in possession
of something to withhold

whistle down a star

he lay there for a week
not even his sapphire eyes
drew vultures or coyotes

and when he had rested
he stuck a lily in his hair
and whistled down a star

consort with coroners

loud wounds & bagpipes
not enough 5th avenues
for the mortally wounded's
fifes & drums & disarray
not enough spectators
applause & patriotism
for those who wet our lips
with their bile & blood
whistles & white gloves
trumpets & sunny despair
and behind these
barricades
who can apologize enough
or understand for what
we are all coroners

fill in the blanks

darkly we fumble blanks
cats fondle details

darkness is womb woods
navel of an orgasmic sea

and we toothpick sailors
in paper boats

dream fresneled light
to show us phantasms

called destinations
sometimes even home

with 20/20 vision
we sprint on broken glass

smash vitrines and stroke
the wrong foot under the table

yet darkness shelters
us from shards of light

and in the ambiguity we catch
our breath and death of calm

enjoy the creak of ice

not to the sun fanatically
i turn but reassured
a north of here
quells the florid
bacterial writhing
of exhibitionists
& whinge of yammerers

my heliotropic face
lulls you to forget
arctic hurtlings
in every act
but I enjoy this creak
of ice to equatorial
& teeming rot

remember marilyn

what i want will not be *there*
any more than horizon is
because there is a mirage

and no *there's no there* where i am going
nor anywhere where i get
because all i see is in back of my eyes

i have nowhere to go or get
and blink and melt
horizons off my eyelashes

but if there were a there
i would know it by the warmth
of your hand in mine

and be dogged to the last

you are witnesses fireflies
fleeting things otherlings
witness i was dogged here
in the service of someone else's eyes
and now have gone to drink their tears

# of this and it

i'm not afraid of this
(god caught in my teeth)
but it's another matter
a dirty incision compared
to the innards of a peach

this is a celebration
it is a wicked guest
whom i'd gladly kill
while sparing mice
and if i don't use italics

to show you what i mean
it simply means I'm pouring
volatile stuff in my lab
and don't want to quibble
about dangers to the tongue
poised between the teeth

and i've already told you
how much i know about god
and how much i distrust it
in all its manifestations
compared to this

evensong

evensong

1

you are a blue heron at dusk
savoring night's refreshments
stitching one spectral dimension
to another seamlessly

you are the curtain closing
without you the fabric tears
light riots in the wounds
of the great dark beast

trailing its cloak across
the impertinences of the day
nothing is as needed or dread
as you, nor as forlorn

and if i knew who you are
i wouldn't think you clutch
the tatters of my life
as you daub the bloody sun

watching you i choke
on the namelessness of things
you are the ancient sob
with which I learned to live

2

if something is behind or under everything
on what can we depend? if we can remove them
but not live with them, if they threaten us
what space is there between pronouns
or between life and death? If we go there
what is here but a departure point?

3

riding peggy's shoulders, braiding her blonde hair
seemed to promise a happy life

ruin waited just across the gowanus
soon I came to think it always would.

who would have thought this child aloft
in a wind goddess's hands
would plunge obsessed
by the shadow of the heron?

4

in paper ships
burn eventualities
i have no use for them
insurance is too high
tariffs too steep
but a man without them
where has he to go
except to be an ashen sheet
on a pond transected
by a heron's leaving?

5

submerged in ourselves
we read each others' signatures
and make ready for denial

6

who would have thought
you would crash me on the street
even though i move out of your way
because my enemy signature
a signal so familiar to you
that no matter how i look
you know me for what i am
drives you to collide
with the other lives you've lived
their flotsam baffling
your commission?

7

i dream in my old age
both predator and prey
of departing famished

i can't put on my socks
unless i mimic herons on one foot
and thinking of their elegance fly
from aging's embarrassments

8

what happens when one dies
when we step naked from babel
but the scouring innocence
and surgical light of the child
burning the rags of the world?

there's not much here to miss
but crystal tears cleansing
scars of tortures past
or put another way
nothing here to miss
but a reflection in a puddle
encroached by a tsunami of tar

what is left when one dies
is a color beyond the spectrum

9

i need buckets of blue light
to soak my leaden feet
and get my rhythms back
i have behavioral issues
i'm seasonally challenged
but mostly it's the flowers
in my ruined solarium-head
i worry about

i want sylphs and undines
to mind my fancies till
they're healthy enough
to pollinate and then
like a heron i'll greet
the evening sun

10

he turns to heron form
before my eye can fix him
to live in dusks of mirrors
—changeable country
variable geometry—
going to and fro
up and down
trackless in the snow

he pulls in his shadow
soaks up the light

his journey ear to ear
fills my brain at night
with sounds of corduroy

i don't know who he is
what he bodes but
it does not promise time
to think about it

11

i rise like a buzzard now
or more mercifully
a heron clutching his just desert

i don't perch on rooftops
but i cast a shadow
on the innocent

because lovelier people
transit in back of me
like the sun

we need each other's light
or we'd be as shadowless
and cold as vampires

my back is always to the sun
to see how long my shadow is
or to make sure I have one

12

this carp life spent scoping
the hole in the world
for the shadow of the heron
stops like baroque music
                        presaging nothing

what do i want in the dusk
but that the heron should have a shadow?

and i will surrender that
to wraiths rhyming my name
... *let me speak with them awhile...*

13

he steals over the stream bed
to the funeral of light
i follow him certain
of rest setting in

he knows where he's going
i hardly know where i've been
he's about something to eat
i follow him to find
what i'm about—hungry too

coda

islips of my mind

Were it not for shape memory in my cock
there'd be no queensboro to erect
to the astorias of my desires   the grudgelands
between the towers and the sea would crawl
with honking incidents and sting
the sore carcass of my brain rifling
cardboard suitcases in forsaken attics
in the sunken islips of a childhood
ruined by the itchy fingers of the dead.

A message from Djelloul Marbrook

If you have enjoyed this book both my publisher and I would be grateful if you would leave a short review at *goodreads.com* and/or at the website where you bought this book.

CPSIA information can be obtained
at www.ICGtesting.com
Printed in the USA
BVHW07s1632210718
522150BV00004B/16/P